Crimson and Gold

Ashi Sharma

BookLeaf Publishing

India | USA | UK

Presentation by *BookLeaf Publishing*

Web: www.bookleafpub.com

E-mail: info@bookleafpub.com

ISBN: 9789363312593

First edition 2024

To My Nikki

Your Paw-prints forever remain on my heart

ACKNOWLEDGEMENT

As I stand at the threshold of presenting 'Crimson and Gold' to the world, I am overwhelmed with a profound sense of gratitude for the many souls who have illuminated my path and enriched my journey along the way.

First and foremost, I express my deepest appreciation to my beloved pet, Nikki, whose unconditional love and companionship brought immeasurable joy to my life. Her passing left her paw prints on my heart, inspiring many of the poems within this collection. Nikki's presence continues to resonate within these pages, a testament to the enduring bond between humans and their furry companions, and the profound lessons they impart.

To my dear cousin, Arushi Sharma whose unwavering support and boundless love have been a source of strength and inspiration throughout my life's journey, I offer my heartfelt gratitude. Your presence has been a guiding light, illuminating the darkest corners of my soul and infusing my spirit with hope and resilience.

I also extend my deepest appreciation to my beloved friend, the late Gurdeep Saxena, whose untimely departure during the tumultuous days of the pandemic left an irreplaceable void in my heart. Your memory lives on in the echoes of one of the poems, a testament to the enduring power of friendship and the fragility of life's precious moments.

To my grandmother, my nani, the late great Tara Rani Kalia, whose stories of resilience, hope, optimism, and enthusiasm have always been a wellspring of inspiration, I owe a debt of gratitude that words cannot fully convey. Her life, rich with experiences and wisdom, has been a beacon of light and strength. Her legacy of unwavering positivity and strength in the face of adversity continues to guide my steps and shape my understanding of life's true essence.

My heartfelt thanks go out to my parents, my mother Shabnam Sharma and my father Brij Bhushan Sharma. Their unwavering support and encouragement have been a cornerstone of my journey. No matter how unconventional or out-of-the-box my projects have been, they have always stood by me with love and enthusiasm. Their belief in my dreams and their constant reassurance have provided the foundation upon which I have built my creative endeavours.

I am deeply grateful to Rupi Kaur, whose work has had a profound influence on my writing. Her book, Healing Through Words, has been a huge catalyst for my expression and healing. Many of the poems in this collection have emerged from the exercises and prompts she provided, helping me to navigate the depths of my emotions and transform them into art.

To my family and friends, whose steadfast belief in my creative endeavours has sustained me through the highs and lows of the writing process, I am eternally grateful. Your unwavering support has been a beacon of light, guiding me through the darkest nights and inspiring me to persevere in pursuit of my dreams.

I am deeply indebted to my readers, whose open hearts and receptive minds have embraced the words contained within these pages. Your willingness to embark on this journey with me, to explore the depths of human emotion and the transformative power of healing, fills me with humility and gratitude.

To the countless poets, writers, and artists whose works have inspired and influenced my own creative expression, I offer my sincerest thanks. Your words have been a source of comfort, inspiration, and solace, guiding me through the labyrinth of my own emotions and illuminating the path toward self-discovery and healing.

Last but not least, I extend my heartfelt appreciation to the universe itself, whose infinite wisdom and boundless creativity infuse every word, every line, every verse of 'Crimson and Gold' with the essence of life itself. May these poems serve as a tribute to the beauty and resilience of the human spirit, and a beacon of hope for all who journey through the depths of emotion and the heights of healing.

PREFACE

Emotions are the threads that weave together the fabric of our lives. They shape our experiences, colour our perceptions, and guide our journey throughout our existence. In this collection of poetry, I invite you to embark on a deeply personal exploration of these emotions (both heavy and light) and the transformative power of healing.

For me, poetry has always been a sanctuary where I can pour out the depths of my soul, unfiltered and unadorned. Each poem in this collection is a fragment of my journey, a whisper from the heart, an echo of the soul. I have sought to capture the raw, unbridled essence of human emotion, painting with words the myriad shades of passion, sorrow, anger, grief, love, healing and ultimately transformation.

The title, 'Crimson and Gold', was not chosen lightly. It represents the dichotomy of human experiences, the interplay between darkness and light, pain and healing, despair and hope. Crimson symbolises the raw, unyielding power of our emotions that courses through our veins like fire. It speaks to the depths of our suffering, the weight of our burdens, and the tumultuous storms that rage within us.

And yet, amidst the crimson, there is a beacon of golden light, a promise of redemption. Gold symbolises the transformative power of healing. The alchemy of the soul that turns pain into wisdom, and suffering into strength. It represents the moments of clarity, the glimmers of hope, and the quiet resilience that lies within each of us.

May 'Crimson and Gold' serve as a guiding light, a source of comfort, inspiration, and solace in times of darkness. May it remind you that even in the depths of despair, there is always hope, that even in the darkest night, there is always a glimmer of dawn on the horizon.

With deepest gratitude and warmest wishes,
Ashi Sharma

Emotions that we
Fail to understand truly
Drive our lifetimes

Unwrapping the Gift Of Anger

Today anger raged in me
out of nowhere wild and free
I was taken aback by surprise
it seemed it had a lot to hide

So I sat down with its layers
the dark night of the soul was declared
unwrapping and discovered
overwhelmed in despair

It started with a lot of blame
that I put on others
like I was a victim
in an unfair game

With the victim, I sat
a little while longer
saw my part in the suffering
and it started to bother

Decided that I want to change
saw guilt in its full range
for all the people I threw
under the bus

to protect myself
and made a huge fuss

These people loved and trusted me
I took them for granted
for what they give so unconditionally
and when the same happened to me
here I lay on the ground
crying like a small baby

So I apologised
for my mistakes
and met shame
before the dawn breaks

I was ashamed I have become
this porcupine and so numb
Absolutely blind that I couldn't see
I hurt people all around me

Then grief came
at the break of dawn
this is not what I want
away I have been running hastily
damaging beautiful connections greatly

Labelling situations, places as bored
pushed people away
like pawns off of a chess board

and all they ever wanted for me
was to give and receive love freely

Family, lovers, colleagues and friends
the ones who are and the ones who left
now how clearly I see
my avoidance is my own misery

As the sun rises again
illuminates my darkness within
wait how did I start here then
was it really just anger
Tell me, again?

Cemented With Sadness and Pain

In an abandoned ally
torn and forgotten
pissed at, rewarded with
dirt and garbage
for being vocal about abuse
all my feelings were
buried like I am a brick wall
failing to notice
that bricks are made of
the colour red
and a wall does have ears
if not a mouth to speak.

Surrender

For many years
I didn't feel
feel a single thing
for there are deep
deep wounds inside somewhere
which cause me this pain
as soon as I try to feel
all the things which I have been
through rough times
which make my heart bleed

Today after so long
when I opened my heart
I saw one of the wounds
and I ran to my tarot cards
shuffled them, said a prayer
hoping it will make me aware
of 'how shall I heal this wound?'
Stitch it up?
Or let it loose?

Asked these questions
and laid my cards
on the table and
stared for an hour

contemplating how to
ask this question again
"Is this love? No, it ain't."
I gathered some courage
from somewhere
to make all my doubts disappear

Picked a card
'Trust,' it said...
and I decided to jump off
in the mystery of the unknown
and as I fell
my heart beat rose
for I don't know
where will I land

How does it matter?
Now it is out of my hand
I have surrendered
to the unknown
What will happen?
Only the almighty knows.

My Soul Has Seen it All

My soul has seen it all...
When I slept in the lap
of Mother Nature
when trees were her fingers
and the grassland her lap

When the blossoms
showed her love for me
and rains were her pain
when hot lava was her anger
and the pleasant winds her joy

When I called her
my very own mother
and she treated me
as her own sweet child
she gave me a warm place to sleep
and nutritious food
when hunger made me blind

I worshipped her for who she is
and she accepted me as I am
we had a beautiful bond with each other

now it all feels like a beautiful dream
When I look at this world today
"It has been a zillion years!" I think
I have this knowing in my soul
Because it has seen it all

My eyes can clearly see that
the landscape now has changed
when I close my eyes
I see my mother
feel her connection the same way
but when I open them
she looks in so much pain...

Love is Not Enough

Love is not enough
to walk the path
it needs to be grounded
rooted in self-esteem
the one you look for
is not responsible
for your happiness
and well-being.

It is up to oneself
to be a whole being,
a complete individual.
Share who you are
meet the one in your entirety.

Strength from within
a foundation firm
with trust and belief
our spirits affirm
no need to please
convince or conform.

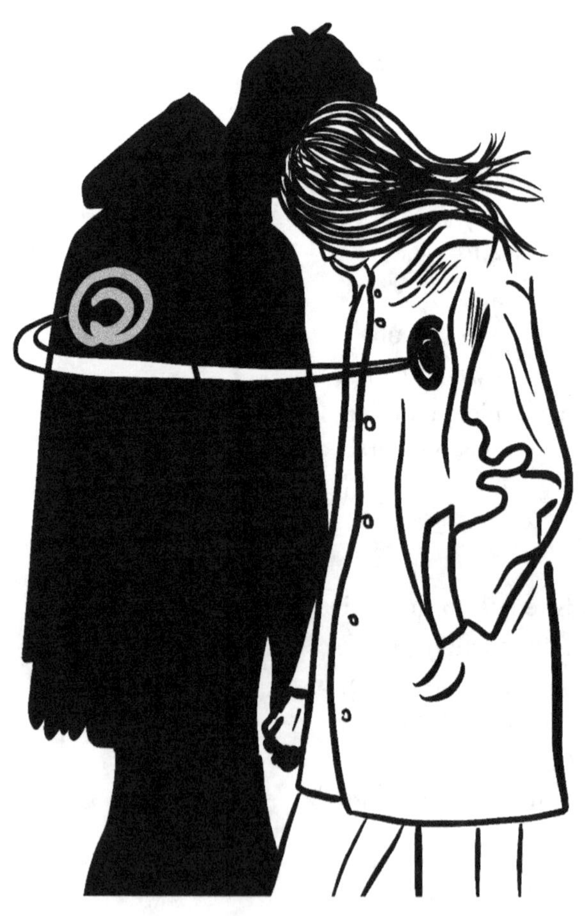

Unabridged in unity
together we rise
with hearts intertwined
yet individually strong
in body and mind
enchantment of the divine.

Spirit Alive

Sparkling stars
shiny Moon
candlelight
a bunch of herbs
filled water
In a cup
with incense of rosewood

Crystal wands
sacred space
some flowers
and their essence

That is all
what we need
to connect with our Goddess
a ritual in progress

Inside-out
cleansing begins
as we start to dance and chant
heart and drums
with our feet
aligning with the
rhythmic life

that is all
what we need
to rid us of our stress

Intoxicated
in the breath of life
lost in the feeling
of feeling so alive

That is all
what we need
to connect to the being inside

Happy-high
nature worshippers
All across the world, we are

Ignorance and jealousy
took over some completely
and they though
oh what fun
would it be to bring in Patriarchy

So they set on fire
Burnt us all
Locked us in
if we survived
thinking that

it can now kill us
and they'll never
see us again

That is all
what they could do
blinded by their wish to rule
and in this way
they didn't know
not our bodies
but in our spirits
we live and are alive.

And it is
Always
Going to stay
Alive…

Celestial lights

The star of Venus visible from the valley
Reborn, coming out of her veil
Escaped the jaws of a viper
After voyaging from vertical volcanos
Bestowing her violet healing light
Opening vaults of prosperity
On her vehicle filling void vases
Wife of Vulcan, lord of flames
Serving vultures and vampires the same.

Vesta-Bestowing Homes

24

Goddess Vesta a Virgo
Prospering devotees with vegetation and vine
Worshipped in homes and in temples
Protects mothers and virgins alike

Enigma of Valkyries

26

The Valkyries arriving on their horses
On the gates of Valhalla, a vulva opens
VITRIOL, if you decode it
The Vajra, in your hand
You hold it.

The little raindrops
Relieved sorrow's broken pain
Emerging Relief

The Art of Healing
Self-Sabotage

We want love
and we want love to stay
but no matter what we do
it keeps getting further away

For love is allowing someone to see
how much our insides bleed
but how can we let them see
what we ourselves are not ready to believe

So we build around
all these walls
high and strong
almost impossible to fall

You see but love is like a wrecking ball
it hits us suddenly and hard
and all our strong walls
simply crumble and fall

And it hurts us so deep
for our wounds come to light
our insecurities drip
from our beings naked and tight

staying confined to our walls
makes us hard as the boulder that falls

So we blame love
and the one who carries it
shame them, shun them
shut them out
because they dared to say out
loud and clear what they feel
dared to bring out
all these hidden insecurities

Grief, guilt, apathy, anger
pride, stress, shame, desire
pain in a coffin with trauma and fear
buried in our bodies frozen
as if the body is a morgue unspoken

For all the memories of our past
that we wanted to forever last
and all the ugliness we conceal
internalise, guild, hide and shield
all the pests we souvenir
in an attic, by magic
expect it all to disappear

It is not easy to affirm
that we are not as perfect
as we had come

or pretend to be
that feeling is eerie

Follow this feeling
and you will see
it opens new doors
abundant oceans and seas
a life of endless possibilities
heal this self-sabotage
and set yourself free.

Home a Place To Be

She took me in when I had no hopes left
She took me in when I was at my lowest
She took me in when I had nowhere to go
She took me in when I had no place to call home
She took me in and gave all she could
possibly give and gave even more
She took me in even if it meant being at war
She took me in and shared with me everything
she had
She took me in as I was, whether things were
good or bad
She took me in and shared her warm, fuzzy heart
She took me in and made me paint wall art
She took me in and opened herself to me
She took me in and showed me endless
possibilities
She took me in opened my eyes and heart
She took me in and showed me who I am, can be
and what I am not
She took me in and she wrote sonnets
She took me in and now I am a poet
She took me in and made me feel safe
I cannot even describe her warm embrace
because of her, now my soul knows
what it really feels like to be at home.

Being Illuminated

I am a light
I shine bright
first I was afraid
but now I realise
It is not me
to dim my shine
it is other's insecurities
that needs to be illuminated
with my glare
I burn bright
don't let a small chapter
define your whole life
have the courage
to write what you want
even when you are disliked
you always have the power
to choose what is right
the only reason you are stuck
is—you don't think you might
so get out of the way
follow the will of divine
your boundaries are your quests
Break, Heal, Rise.

The One Who Deserves

I will not accept
scrapes, crumbs and shreds
inconsistency, absence and gaslight
for I seek the whole
not the fragments and dregs

I am too healed to settle
for the leftovers being served
safety, reassurance, commitment
communication and consistency
a life full and rich
not half-measured, bereft
of dreams, hopes and love

In abundance, not theft
Love doesn't need to beg
freely love I serve
me, the one who deserves
divined will be by destiny
guided by the stars' reserve
a healed one will emerge.

Mirror's Alchemy

This morning, I woke up
something had changed
the mirror was unbroken
with no signs of disdain

The face in the past
reminded me of the hurt
was now looking flawless
love and compassion unearthed

How harsh have I been
and put on these masks
just so I don't notice
them imperfections and scars

When I let go of
the veil and disguise
what I thought
I'm supposed to be
who can excel and thrive

I decided no more will I hide
all that I am
learnt to embody and imbibe
Personification to be done from the inside

Alchemy of inner terrain
places where I want to go
places where I have been
a moment to cherish and struggles cease

I see in the mirror clearly
love what I see so dearly
adventures odyssey certainly
here I arrive, so it be.

The Demands of Grief

Grief is a five letter word
a number that represents freedom
yet look at the irony
grief to the past keeps imprisoned

Grief demands to be felt
and it brings along all the memories
spent together in love and in misery
feeling it changes life's trajectory

All coulda woulda shoulda's
keep rising and falling like waves
until it all seems in haze
the beloved is cremated or in grave

We try to weep it out
the pain we feel guts about
all the grudges, regrets and incomplete
conversations, wishes and deeds

Grief then takes you deep
scattered dots and creed
questions what we have done
and all that is yet to come

When you deny meeting grief
you deny the present reality
the more you stay in denial
grief becomes a painful trial

It changes forms indeed
anger in you, lives and breeds
confuses you, how to deal
layers and layers to peel

One day just find the courage
face fears and pay your homage
allowing yourself to grieve
is allowing yourself to heal

That is all grief demands
Acceptance of what is
and what is not
gifts you with inner harmony
simply then it sets you free.

Error 404- Page Not Found

My teenage heart mourns a loss
Love notes written, I never got
Dried flowers couldn't bury in books
Exchanging side-eyed shy looks
From a connection, innocent and deep
That I always wanted profound
But unfortunately never found

If You Ever Were In Love With Me

Everyone who has ever thought
you are in love with me
for you don't see the flawed me
that I encounter daily

Gratitude from the bottom of my heart
for your courage to express
your true feelings with me
a reminder—loveable I am

Even when I don't see it
and to those who wanted to possess
may the parts of you that came
to seek healing, solace and completion
all in the name of love

May you be mended once and for all
for I am a burning flame
living, breathing, healing fire
and for the rest too afraid to accept
when I offered its depths
May you see yet
the worthiness, potential and possibilities

scare, overwhelm, fears in you erect
Choice you make to run away
hide yourself or push away
may you heal one day
see how perfect you are
when you are wishing upon a star
worthy you are of what you seek
yet so afraid, fight, flee or freeze
May your fragments integrate and heal.

Life I Live

When no one is looking
I am a little too harsh on me
always trying to march to perfection
and that brings me to honesty

I do my work with
an attitude of joy
it brings me inner satisfaction
without which life feels empty

In the past
I used to worry
about me and my journey
what others might think

It took some time to realise
learn to be gentle with me
my life is for me to live
being who I am in this world
I have so much to give

I do things in ace
at my own glacial pace
it is a real luxury in life
for some, my peace annoy
Life at my own pace I enjoy.

Treasure Hunt

I was convinced that
you are the one for me
my life with you
I could visualise so clearly
the time I spent with you
life flowed effortlessly
I forgot in those moments
all about my misery
it was the friendship
the familiarity that
drew me in deep
How silently in my heart
You slipped in
I had no plans
of falling for someone remotely
I was not really looking
and damn I spiralled jolty

Love unexpected, a connection grew
in messages and calls
it all felt so true
but when I asked
what we are
are we friends
or something has come too far

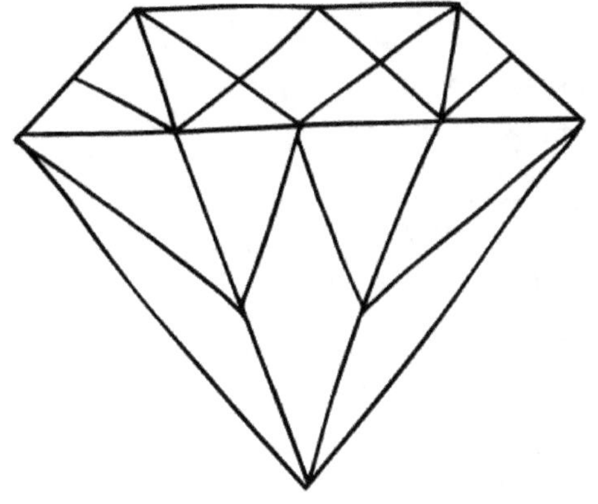

you said you are confused
what do you want
where do you want to go
the next things I saw
you were forging connections
In different cities
chasing new attractions
here I stand asking questions
was it real at all
Or all what I imagined

Now I realise
It is all a means
to hide from your fears
shades and shadows
You are just
passing your time
waiting for your past
to realign
or someone to confine

But I am not a waiting room
neither an entertainment spot
Nor a spa or a salon

I am a treasure hunt
unearth my depths
with patience and care
which demands commitment

a rare lifetime affair
through adventure quests
my heart you may find
a journey worth taking
true love intertwined
a love so rare and fair
journey through lows and highs
seek with earnest intent
only then you find
the heart I present.

Parts and Pieces Of Forgiveness

Today, I forgive a part of me
for feeling not good enough
even when I gave all of me
and still, it was not enough

I forgive the part that gave up
when the going got tough
I did my best but didn't get through
took some lies to be the truth

I forgive myself for not realising
my own insecurities
I blamed, projected, sabotaged
others for my atrocities

My insecurities and fears
subconsciously self-destruct
progress and growth end up obstruct
creates a deep sense of distrust

When I sat and saw
the drama of my own
started recognising patterns
repeating on and on and on

Tired of being chained
to this painful rhythm
'this needs to change!'
I decided to forgive
started to beat my own drum

On the journey to this change
certainly made a lot of mistakes
forgiving very same mistakes
became a catalyst to further change

Kept myself on my path
even when times were dark
stayed true to my fire and spark
that is why I am a Blazing Star.

You are in their Heart

You know, you are in their heart
When you had spent
Some time apart
Something feels vacant

When they see you again
You don't ask
They still tell you where
They have been doing, when and what

They spill all the tea in detail
Make sure to blaze
Every conversation trail
At a glacial pace

But the time flies so fast
You lose the conversations last
And it's time to go home
A little more they want to roam

The twinkle in their eye
When you say bye-bye
It all becomes so clear
You are their dear

Letting fall apart
Was all that really needed
For it to be perfect

Spiralling Endlessly

The cracks in the thoughts
Directionless going in spirals
What time is it?
What was I doing with this pen in my hand?
How long has it been,
Since I was staring into space?
Wait, where am I?
When did I get here in the first place?

Frozen in space and time
Trying to make sense
Of the fragmented pieces
Of memories and incidences
Blurred and blacked out
Coming and going in phases
Constantly in self-doubt
Stuck in self-blame

Trying to somehow
Shove it in a mental closet
Stuff it and forget it
Become a high-achiever
Fruitless actions in vain
One triggering incidence after another
Or a single setback

All that I build up, comes crumbling down

Closet overflowing, in my face
Right in front of me
Scattered on the surface
Of all the achievements and happiness
Anger boils up
Whatever was under the rug
A violent volcano erupts

It wants to right all the wrongs
Injustices the eyes have ever seen
And now I am blinded
The present I cannot see
My head starts spinning
Spiralling in space endlessly
Clueless broken brain
The head detaches from the body

This is all my fault
Hellow Anxiety
The cracks in the thoughts
Directionless going in spirals
Wait, what time is it?
What was I doing with this pen in my hand?
How long has it been?

I Will always Remember You

Looking out the window
today of my flight
I saw these beautiful golden clouds
as I touched your soft fuzzy fur, so nice
flying above these clouds
hoping will catch a view
for now, you are a part of heaven
the clouds your home anew
maybe you are somewhere
frolicking wild and free
on the rainbow or way beyond
where no mind can reach
or maybe you are among the stars
twinkling like your eyes
or perhaps you are a solar storm
like your helicopter tail wags vigorous haywire
maybe you are preparing
somewhere to be reborn too
till next we meet
I will always remember you.

– A tribute to Nikki

Nani

I remember your stories narrated
I would sit and listen beside your bed
It all felt so random back then
Now when I look back to make sense
They all are priceless gems

You gave us the most precious heirlooms
Your sheer presence was a blessing and a boon
Your smile and warm welcomes
Yummy delicious food, a mandated custom
When you spoke, there was no scope for
boredom

Your love for Limca and sweets
Your chubby cheeks like red beets
You always made sure together family gathers
Share and celebrate everything together
Through thick and thin come what no matter

I know you are in a better place
Protecting us, sending all the grace
You lived an absolute full life
Taught us to do the same
With all our might
We shine bright like a flame

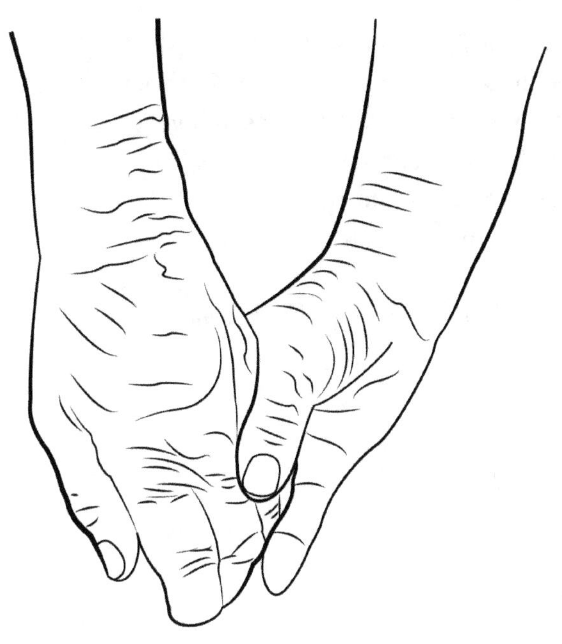

Feel honoured to carry on your legacy

Your wisdom and strength
You are my ancestor, a guiding star
Though distant, you are never far
Through generations, your spirit flows
In our hearts, your memory grows

In your footsteps, we tread
With courage and grace, never misled
Strive to live by the lessons you gave
To honour your name
The values you instilled
The path you paved

-A tribute to My Nani, Tara Rani Kalia

Friends Forever

I sat down with my tarot cards
While shuffling, a card jumped out
Face down on the floor
6 of cups, wanted to sprout

Immediately, transported my heart
To the time I was practising this art
We sat down and did it together for hours
Tea, snacks and incense of flowers

Your wisdom you shared with me, my friend
Your experience made my broken heart mend
Even our ages years apart
Effortless it was to associate
Since forever as we were playmates

Whenever I had boy troubles
You always offered your wise bubbles
That would burst my troubles away
The bubbles are now diamonds
 In my heart, they stay

In your final hours when I got a call
I sat to send you prayers and healing
Before the night falls

In visions, you said, "Don't you worry about me.
I will be alright soon, you'll see."

Soon I saw you surrounded by light
You were all covered in fireflies
And then the fireflies flew away
Leaving behind only memories that stay

I still think about you sometimes
When I am stuck in my life
Always think what you would say
That will make worries go away

Here I am writing poetry too
Maybe not as good as you
I wish you could tell me how I did
Your sageness was a light that never hid

In silence, I feel you cheer
Encouraging words I can't though hear
Guided by your unseen hand
I write with hope, as once you planned

Each verse, a tribute to your grace
In every line, I see your face
Though distant, yet so near
In every word, you reappear.

-A tribute to my beloved friend, Gurdeep Saxena

Trust

Trust is fragile
If controlled by anxiety
It always waits for
The other shoe to drop
Destined to be broken

Trust is non-existent
If blinded by fear
It is a battle lost
Before it even ever began
Always feeling the world is unfair

Trust is conditional
If served with anger
It is always fighting
Injustice till eternity
Destroying everything along the way

Trust is dangerous
It requires vulnerability
Which means the possibility
To risk oneself to get hurt
Pain it can blurt

Trust is healing
If paired with hope
Gives birth to miracles
With it, love prevails
From life darkness assails.

A Multipotentialite's Mind

How does an opal choose its flares?
When you ask me to pick (a)part
My mind is like a foetus on flames
I have to integrate so much art

When you ask me to pick (a)part
Gracefulness cannot be fragmented from grace
I have to integrate so much art
Can beauty really choose its face?

Gracefulness cannot be fragmented from grace
Ideas in my head flow like a fountain
Can beauty really choose its face?
But to make a fortune is to climb a mountain

Ideas in my head flow like a fountain
Trying to find intersections of Dahlia flowers
But to make a fortune is to climb a mountain
Multipotentialite—a fortress with weird towers

Trying to find intersections of Dahlia flowers
Pickup 5 things in no specific order
Multipotentialite- A fortress with weird towers
With a different flag in every corner

Pickup 5 things in no specific order
A flamingo doesn't single out its feathers in a
fight
With a different flag in every corner
A falcon is never apart from its flight

A flamingo doesn't single out its feathers in a
fight
Trailblazers following our own footprints
A falcon is never apart from its flight
Integrating a diamond with unions and tangents

Trailblazers following our own footprints
My mind is like a foetus on flames
Integrating a diamond with unions and tangents
How does an opal choose its flares?

Vice Victimhood

Dear life, I burn, from ashes, I rise
Though I feel lost, here I have survived
Burdens gone, now I can touch the skies
My ego is broken, here I am so alive

I build up and break and build break
The storms and tides knock over my boat
Yet my spirit remains unshaken
Amidst the storms, I remain afloat

Now I let go of my struggles and blues
I have had enough of this victimhood
In empowerment, I find golden hues
As wounds and fragments heal from my
childhood.

Blessings in disguise all around I see
Breaking generational curses set me free.

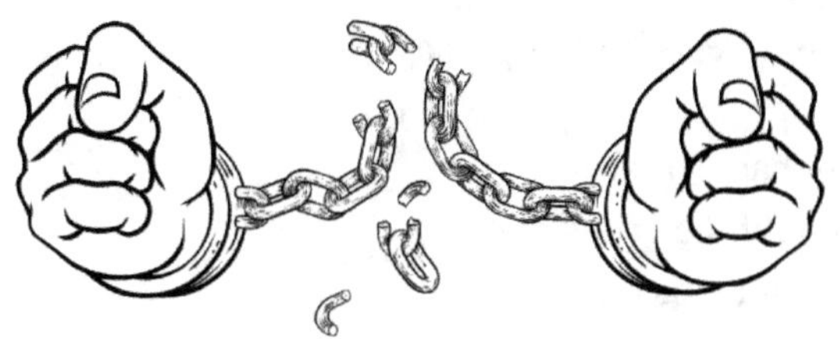

From Crimson To Gold

Crack in my chest
crimson light appears
started spreading across
my entire body

After a while
I realised and saw
pain emerged
as my heart started to thaw

My hands rushed
to hold the crimson crack
dripping agony appeared
tried to pause with a smack

Why me?
I screamed out loud
what have I done
to serve this in a crowd

Staying miserable for a while
decided to finally end the trial
no more a victim will I be
of circumstances or past deeds

There is always a way out
take a step back to look
be done scream and shout
determine, put down your foot

This ends here, draw the line
in compassion yourself you hold
with awareness, your life you mold
Enlightenment turns the Crimson to Gold.

Crimson bleeding wounds
With healing and acceptance
Transmute and ooze Gold

NOTES

NOTES

NOTES

NOTES

NOTES